Original title:
Violets and Visions

Copyright © 2025 Creative Arts Management OÜ
All rights reserved.

Author: Gabriel Kingsley
ISBN HARDBACK: 978-1-80566-741-4
ISBN PAPERBACK: 978-1-80566-870-1

Fantasies in Flora

In a garden of giggles, blooms take flight,
Dancing in sunlight, oh what a sight!
Petals in polka-dots, twirling like fools,
Whispers of laughter break all the rules.

A bee wearing glasses, buzzes with flair,
Telling the flowers, "Life's better with hair!"
The tulips are tickled, the daisies will chuckle,
As petals make puns in the warm summer buckle.

A snappy old rose, with jokes up its seam,
Says, "Roses are red, but I'm just a meme!"
The lilacs roll in laughter, oh what a show,
As sunflowers dance, in a radiant glow.

Even the weeds join in with a grin,
They twist and they twirl, letting chaos begin!
In this playful patch, humor's the king,
Where flowers are jesters, and joy is the spring.

Celestial Gardens

In a patch of purple hue,
The dancing gnomes ask, 'Who knew?'
They sip tea from a flying cup,
And giggle as the stars come up.

Butterflies wear tiny shoes,
And gossip with the morning dews.
A squirrel in a top hat struts,
While a daffodil does ballet nuts.

Beyond the Ferns

A toucan sports an aviator cap,
While frogs in tuxedos take a nap.
The sunflowers play hide and seek,
While ants wear shades, looking sleek.

A hedgehog makes a pie so round,
With jelly beans he's proudly found.
While a snake in a bow tie twirls,
Around the squirrels and their pearls.

Night Blooms and Daydreams

Moonlight sprinkles glittery dust,
As peacocks strut and show off rust.
The lilies wear shoes made of cheese,
While nightingales politely sneeze.

A raccoon steals a slice of pie,
And eats while watching nearby.
With fireflies as disco lights,
The garden parties through the nights.

An Abundance of Echoes

In the meadow, a jester hops,
With daisies woven into props.
A rabbit juggles grapes too bold,
While laughing at the flowers' mold.

Echoes jump from bloom to bloom,
Tickling frogs wake from their gloom.
A warbler leads the merry song,
As the sun bursts forth all day long.

Gaze of the Fading Sun

Beneath the sky, a quirky show,
The sun slides down, a glowing low.
A pigeon struts, with quite the flair,
While squirrels plot, in secret lairs.

A dance of shadows, all around,
The cat thinks it's a royal crown.
The glow of dusk, a playful tease,
As giggles ride the gentle breeze.

Shades of a Quiet Serenade

In twilight's charm, a whisper hums,
While daisies dance to bumblebee drums.
A rooster crows, he missed his cue,
The moon just chuckles, waiting for you.

A frog takes pride, on a lily pad,
Croaking a tune, oh isn't he glad?
The stars begin to twinkle and sway,
As night unfolds, in the funniest way.

Blossoms in a Mystic Breeze

Petals fluttering, a clumsy kite,
While butterflies munch on snacks at night.
A ladybug slips, a silent shout,
But giggles grow loud with all the clout.

The daffodils wear hats of cheese,
While ants juggle crumbs with utmost ease.
Nature's jesters, a lively crew,
In a world of whimsy, just for you.

Enchanted Hues of Reflections

Ripples dance on the pond's smooth face,
A fish pops up—oh, what a race!
The frogs and ducks have bets to place,
In water's mirror, the silliness finds space.

A dragonfly stumbles, caught in a spin,
As laughter echoes from within.
The light shows off its vibrant flair,
In shades of giggles filling the air.

Echoing Blooms

In a garden of giggles, petals chuckle light,
Colorful whispers are a comical sight.
Bees wear tiny hats, buzzing tunes of cheer,
Flowers dance wildly, no sign of fear.

Butterflies in tuxedos, prancing with flair,
Snickering petals, floating in the air.
They joke with the sun, in a dazzling show,
Dragging the clouds for the best comedy flow.

Flora's Mystery

In the midst of greens, a riddle does sprout,
A daisy thinks it's a weed, that's no doubt.
Roses gossip wildly, with petals all prim,
While daffodils laugh, oh so bright and slim.

A tulip in pajamas, takes a cozy nap,
While dandelions form a secret map.
Whispers of thyme make the garden scheme,
With herbs conniving, like a wild dream.

Shadows of Blooming Journeys

In the land of patches, shadows stretch long,
Petals plotting mischief, singing a song.
Sunflowers peep out, with jokes up their sleeves,
Tickling the grass while a spider weaves.

Worms twirl in tunnels, giggling below,
The daisies throw parties, they steal the show.
Each stem has a story, each bloom has a tale,
As chaos unfolds on the colorful trail.

The Allure of Purple Haze

In fields where laughter meets the sweet mystique,
   Purple tales linger, with a vibrant streak.
  Giggling with daisies, they jazz up the scene,
   Drunk on the nectar, like a party serene.

   Lavender whispers, "Join the parade!"
  Flailing in flower hats, they're unafraid.
The breeze tells a joke, which makes petals sway,
In the realm of the humorous, come dance and play.

The Light of Flowering Paths

In the meadow, bees do buzz,
Chasing dreams, just because.
Flowers prance, in shadows play,
While the grass insists on sway.

Tickled by the sun's bright cheer,
Worms decide to dance, oh dear!
Daisy hats on bumble's head,
Laughing loud, till dreams are spread.

Frogs in suits take to the stage,
Ribbiting lines, a frog's engage.
Critters gossip, the day's delight,
In a whirl of floral light.

Jolly petals share a joke,
As the breeze begins to poke.
Nature's giggles, soft and spry,
Underneath the endless sky.

Radiance in the Garden

In a plot where colors clash,
Gnomes are caught in silly flash.
Sunflowers wear the silliest frowns,
While tomatoes sport tiny crowns.

Ladybugs debating fate,
Are we insects or just great?
With tiny suits and shoes so bright,
They banter through the sunny light.

Zinnias flirt in floral gowns,
Hoping to catch the bees' renowns.
But the daisies steal the show,
Outrageously, what a glow!

Oh, how the snails all slide and sway,
With sticky trails, they dance all day.
Each petal's laugh, a friendly tease,
In this garden, joy's the breeze.

The Language of Petals

Whispers float on fragrant air,
Petals gossip without a care.
Each bloom shares a funny tale,
Of the grasshopper's great fail.

Butterflies in vibrant hues,
Sporting patterns like tattooed shoes.
Flirting with the leaves nearby,
While sparrows tease in response, oh my!

A tulip trips, a laugh erupts,
As hedgehogs ponder taxes, abrupt.
Bumbling bees, all in a rush,
Miss their dates—oh such a hush!

Petal and leaf in jest collide,
Working hard to turn the tide.
With every giggle, nature sings,
In this world of silly things.

Echoing in the Blue

Under skies of endless charm,
Clouds float by, all soft and warm.
A parrot talks, spills the tea,
While ants plot a wild jubilee.

Blue bells ring with silly tone,
Resisting plans to be alone.
Dandelions with seeds in tow,
Dream of places they will go.

A squirrel with a cheeky grin,
Stashes acorns, thinks to win.
But they roll away, oh what a sight!
Chasing them 'til there's moonlight.

Laughter echoes, breezes tease,
While slip-ups dance upon the leaves.
Nature's humor, bright and true,
In every shade of joyful blue.

Boundless Colors

In a garden of mischief, hues brightly collide,
Daisies in bow ties, with a sunflower guide.
A bluebird's in flip-flops, dancing in the sun,
While squirrels play poker, oh what quirky fun!

Tulips wear top hats, strutting with great flair,
Bees buzz in rhythm, a polka in the air.
The roses all giggle, such chatter they share,
As petals start prancing, without any care.

Night Perfumes

When shadows stretch long and the moon shines bright,
The breezes laugh softly, bringing scents of delight.
A cat in a cape, with a mischievous meow,
Declares midnight snacks whilst performing a bow.

Crickets hold concerts, in fields filled with cheer,
While fireflies waltz, like small chandeliers.
With scents of sweet jasmine, teasing the night,
In this cheeky soirée, everything feels right.

A Glance into Wonderland

Through the looking glass, what a silly sight!
Rabbits in suits argue till the morning light.
A queen with her tarts, in a pastry parade,
While mice juggle cheeses — how can this be played?

Cheshire cat giggles, as he fades in and out,
He gives a sly wink, then starts dancing about.
With croquet mallets, flamingos take the stage,
In this whimsical land, all are filled with gage.

Threads of Nature's Muse

Stitching together the fabric of fun,
With yarn spun from laughter, we weave one by one.
A spider in spectacles, counting each thread,
While daisies knit hats for the bugs in their bed.

Colors entwine, like a dance in the breeze,
As ladybugs sketch with the greatest of ease.
Through stitches of sunlight, the day gets all dressed,
In this playful tapestry, we're truly blessed.

Fading Petals of Memory

Once I had a garden, bright and fair,
But gnats threw a party in my favorite chair.
The daisies danced and the roses turned red,
While I swatted away till I fell out of bed.

Now petals are scattered, like socks in a pile,
I can't find a weed, but I can't find my style.
Memories linger like bugs in the air,
But my gardening skills? They just vanish—beware!

Reflections in the Lavender Light

A purple hue spills across the old bog,
I forgot my hat—now I look like a frog.
The mirror reflects all the mischief I've done,
With lilies laughing, oh, isn't it fun?

I slip on the petals, all slippery and sly,
Wishing I could leap like a toad that's nearby.
The sun's winking down, with a twinkling delight,
As I hop my way home in a lavender light.

A Symphony of Dusk and Eden

As night starts to blanket the world in its cloak,
I try to count sheep, but I end up with smoke.
Crickets are tuning their tiny little band,
While I'm on the floor, with a snack in my hand.

Garden gnomes hold a council by night,
Debating if worms taste better with spice.
The moon nods in rhythm, witnessing the game,
As I fall asleep dreaming of asparagus fame.

Odorous Echoes of Tomorrow

The scents of the past drift through my cluttered mind,
Like an old sock left out in the rain, unrefined.
I plan for the future, with cupcakes and flair,
But end up with pickles, oh life's quite a scare!

Whispers of flowers tickle my brain, oh so sweet,
While I ponder my choices, like snacks I must eat.
The echoes of laughter bounce back from the day,
And all that remains is a very loud 'yay!'

Celestial Scented Whispers

In the garden, blooms collide,
With giggles shared, they take a ride.
Pollen tickles, buzzing buzz,
Petals chat like friends because.

Starlight winks, the frogs compete,
In funky hats, they dance their beat.
The daisies giggle, "Look at me!"
While tulips play a game of free.

Blossoms Under the Moonlight

Dancing petals under the glow,
Fireflies laugh, putting on a show.
"Who's the prettiest?" they tease around,
In this wild garden, joy abounds.

The roses coach the daisies near,
"Try to do the moonwalk, dear!"
With a twist and spin, they take that chance,
While shadows sway in a flower dance.

The Realm of Dreaming Flowers

In dreams, the flowers plot and plan,
A secret party—Oh, what a jam!
They wear capes made of morning dew,
Plotting pranks, just me and you.

Sunflowers gossip about the sun,
"Is he bright, or just having fun?"
Each stem sways to the jester's tune,
While petals whisper, "Let's dance till noon!"

Secrets of the Floral Realm

In the floral realm where laughs erupt,
Tulips hold meetings, plans all disrupt.
"Who stole the snacks?" cranky violets fume,
While marigolds giggle, feeling the bloom.

Chasing butterflies, the petals race,
Zooming past, oh, what a chase!
"Last one to the pond must sing a song!"
And with that jest, they whirl along.

Secrets in Bloom

In a garden where giggles grow,
Petals whisper secrets low.
Bees buzz with a cheeky tune,
Sunlight dances, afternoon.

Squirrels wear hats made of leaves,
Plotting pranks, oh how it weaves!
A flower sneezes, pollen flies,
And makes a butterfly cry sighs.

Mysteries in every bud,
A rose spills tea in the mud.
Tulips tell tales of the night,
While daisies giggle in delight.

Finally the moon comes out,
Blossoms chuckle, stars in route.
The garden holds a winking glee,
As laughter blooms in jubilee.

Shades of Illumination

In the light where shadows laugh,
Color plays a silly half.
Chickens dance in bright array,
While daisies join in the fray.

A fuchsia flower on the ground,
Declares it's lost and needs a hound.
Bumblebees wear tiny hats,
Taking strolls with fancy cats.

Sunflowers sport the coolest shades,
While tulips make funny charades.
Petunias hide in big wide hats,
Trying hard to avoid the bats.

Amidst the light of funny shades,
A jesting breeze rolls like cascades.
In this realm of humorous glee,
Life's a play, come laugh with me!

Ephemeral Blossoms

In a world where giggles sprout,
Petals dance, there's no doubt.
Dandelions wear crowns of gold,
A cheerful sight, truth be told.

A tulip ticks like a clock,
While squirrels play with pebbled rock.
The daisies throw a playful fight,
In this whimsical delight.

Butterflies wear polka dots,
As wind juggles, shows off lots.
While roses blush with joy and tease,
It's a joyous game, oh what a breeze!

Even the thorns seem to joke,
In a bouquet that's gone up in smoke.
In fleeting blooms, laughter's sung,
As petals dance, forever young.

The Garden of Dreams

In a dreamscape where smiles parade,
Children play, and worries fade.
Grasshoppers dance in a bridal veil,
Butterflies giggle, oh, without fail.

A pumpkin sings a merry tune,
While tomatoes play hide and swoon.
The carrots march in a mixed line,
Making dinner alight with wine.

In corners where the shadows sleep,
A sneaky snail makes promises keep.
With blossoms wide, they all conspire,
To make a day that won't tire.

In the garden, joy doesn't cease,
Each blooming laugh is a sweet peace.
So wander here, let laughter beam,
Together in this playful dream.

The Essence of Daydreams

In fields where odd thoughts roam,
Butterflies wear hats and combs.
A rabbit plays the bass guitar,
While daisies sing from near and far.

Clouds do somersaults in the sky,
As thinky birds throw marshmallows high.
A sunflower does a silly dance,
Thinking it might just have a chance.

A lazy snail shows off his speed,
Declaring he'll win the next big breed.
He tripled in size, just for a race,
But lost to a turtle in a sleepy face.

Rainbows slide down like a slide,
And puddles invite me for a ride.
In a world where laugh tracks replay,
Daydreams blossom in the silliest way.

Beneath the Indigo Canopy

Underneath the shade of blue,
Unicorns paint themselves anew.
They critique the style of passing trees,
Who just wave back with the greatest of ease.

Squirrels debate the best nut prize,
While turtles in top hats make their wise ties.
Chattering critters hold a grand dance,
Mixing acorns with bright rom-com romance.

When raccoons throw an evening soiree,
They serve punch made of glittery clay.
Foxes are judging—this is no jest,
While owls narrate, "This is the best!"

A sky purpled with whimsical cheer,
Brings laughter, joy, and zero eerie fear.
In this canopy, where oddities play,
Every moment is a brushed palette of clay.

An Odyssey in Petals

In a meadow of peculiar hues,
Where daisies wear socks and moose sing the blues.
A caterpillar pilots a leaf-shaped plane,
While ants form a conga line in the rain.

A butterfly tries on forty-three hats,
Swapping with squirrels who wear fancy spats.
The flowers are giggling, petals all aglow,
As they trade stories of wizards who sow.

With sugar-coated clouds drifting just right,
A bee sets up a bakery, what a sight!
Pollen cupcakes, sweet and puffy,
Make even the grumpiest florals feel fluffy.

The moon drops by with a wink and a nod,
To join in the fun, he's slightly unshod.
As the stars join the chorus, singing so loud,
It's a flower fest that draws quite the crowd!

A Mosaic of Imagination

In a world made of jellybeans and cream,
Marshmallows bounce with a springy beam.
Pineapples sport sunglasses with flair,
As cupcakes twirl through the taste-bud air.

Clouds hold auditions for plays in the sky,
As popcorn trees munch on passersby.
Kites with googly eyes tell silly jokes,
While gingerbread men crack up in smoky cloaks.

A dragon that's purple brews peppermint tea,
As kittens in bowties exchange pleasantries.
In dreamlike corners, odd stories connect,
Crafting laughter from every aspect.

Creativity sparkles in colors so bright,
In this silly realm, everything feels right.
Each twist and turn brings giggles anew,
A whimsical dance where imagination grew.

The Garden of Unseen Spirits

In a garden where shadows giggle,
A cactus told a dandelion jiggle.
The roses played tag with the breeze,
While tulips practiced their stand-up tease.

The lilies wore hats, oh so grand,
And daisies danced hand in hand.
A gopher clown gave a wink,
As butterflies lined up for a drink.

The laughter echoed in the air,
As mushrooms debated their style of hair.
The sunflowers cracked jokes at dawn,
While crickets chirped—a quirky song.

Bees buzzed in as the show went wild,
Claiming to be nature's very own child.
In this garden where humor grew,
Every petal had its own debut.

Reflections in a Petal Mirror

In a dewdrop, a snail made a face,
Claiming he'd win the slowest race.
He slipped and slid with flair and grace,
While butterflies rolled in laughing space.

A ladybug wore shades, looking bright,
Claiming she was the star of the night.
But ants marched in with a funny parade,
A comical show that never would fade.

The mirror of petals, a laughing breeze,
Caught all the pranks that aimed to please.
A dragonfly somersaulted in flight,
While frogs croaked the songs of delight.

In the world of the silly and grand,
Reflection sparked jokes as they planned.
With each ripple, new laughter would bloom,
Creating a festival in every room.

Beyond the Horizon of Color

Beyond where colors swirl and blend,
The sky is a canvas where giggles ascend.
A purple parrot told a tall tale,
As clouds shaped giraffes with a cheeky wail.

In this land where hues come alive,
A rainbow chicken learned to drive.
It crashed through puddles, oh what a sight,
Making rainbows in the light of night.

A jester star with a twinkling cheer,
Gave wishes to dreams that lingered near.
While sunsets punned in shades of gold,
With jokes so funny, they never seemed old.

At dusk, the color wheel spun in delight,
As fireflies chuckled, twinkling so bright.
In this colorful circus, nothing's too odd,
Every hue has its own silly facade.

A Kaleidoscope of Thoughts

In my mind, a jigsaw of laughter and fun,
Thoughts flip and twist like a circus run.
A cat in a hat, juggling fish with grace,
While a penguin tap dances all over the place.

A parade of ideas, silly and mad,
Where a cow on a skateboard looks totally rad.
With each turn of the lens, a new scene beams,
As a unicorn juggles imaginary dreams.

The kaleidoscope spins, a colorful craze,
While thoughts hopscotch through whimsical ways.
A banana serenades a grapefruit song,
In this wild landscape, nothing feels wrong.

From giggles to snorts, the laughter won't stop,
As a balloon dog takes a big, silly hop.
In this swirling madness, joy takes its flight,
Creating a world that's dazzlingly bright.

Secret Gardens of the Heart

In a garden where giggles bloom,
Tiny gnomes hide under the broom,
They debate if grass is really green,
Or if it's just a crazy dream.

Butterflies dance like they're in a play,
While worms wear hats and cheer all day,
A rosebud thinks it can sing a tune,
But only hums like a grumpy raccoon.

Sunshine tickles the petals wide,
As clouds throw pies from up high wide,
Laughter echoes through the leafy maze,
Creating mischief in playful ways.

When night falls, the fireflies come,
Twinkling jokes in a brightened hum,
The secret garden keeps its charm,
With silly antics, it means no harm.

Tales Carried by the Wind

The breeze brings stories spun with yarn,
Of a cat who claims he's a barn,
He wears a hat with a flip and a flop,
And naps in a chair made from a mop.

A dandelion dreams of being a star,
While ants play music on a candy bar,
Each gust of laughter travels afar,
As if the wind knows just who we are.

Marshmallows squeak while floating afloat,
In boats of bread, they happily gloat,
They sail on rivers of fizzy juice,
With laughter making sweet their truce.

When whispers of night begin to hum,
Crickets join in with their tiny drum,
The tales twist in gaps of bright moonlight,
Tickling hearts in the still of the night.

Flagrant Fantasies at Dusk

At dusk, the sky wears fancy shoes,
While oranges mingle with purple hues,
A lazy raccoon sips on sweet tea,
Dreaming he's king of a vast jubilee.

The clouds form shapes, like ice cream cones,
As frogs in tuxedos dance on stones,
Chasing fireflies in a silly spree,
They muse about life as if it's free.

A sleepy bug plays the tiny lute,
Telling tales of his adventures so cute,
In a bog where the lilies gossip and giggle,
Each croak and chirp sends the willows to wiggle.

When shadows stretch like a cat on the prowl,
The moon gives a wink with a mischievous growl,
Dreams take flight as night drapes its shawl,
In whimsical worlds where laughter stands tall.

The Scent of Whispered Time

Tick-tock, the clock does a dance,
While time wears socks that look askance,
The air smells sweet like sugar and cheese,
In moments where whimsy rides the breeze.

A curious pair of old shoes take flight,
Wobbling high in the soft starlight,
They giggle and chatter of places seen,
As they leap through dreams on a trampoline.

Vintage tea cups hold stories so rich,
Spilling secrets with a clink and a hitch,
In the teapot, a world whirls around,
Where teacups gossip and chickens astound.

As night whispers tales to the quiet street,
Laughter rings out in the soft, hazy heat,
A charming aroma lingers, it seems,
In the gentle embrace of our silliest dreams.

A Symphony of Flowers

In a garden where giggles dance,
The daisies join in a playful prance.
Butterflies wear hats quite askew,
While bees hum tunes, oh so very blue.

Petunias gossip, sharing the news,
About the roses and their bright shoes.
Tulips tattle with petals aglow,
While the sun winks, putting on a show.

A daffodil slips on a slippery leaf,
Causing the marigolds to yelp in disbelief.
Laughter spills like nectar in the air,
In this floral concert, who has a care?

So join the waltz beneath the sun's smile,
Where blooms make jokes, all the while.
A symphony of colors and cheer,
In this garden, there's nothing to fear.

Fantasies in Bloom

In a land where the carrots wear crowns,
And the lettuce dances in gowns.
Radishes play peek-a-boo with the sun,
While tomatoes giggle, saying, "Let's run!"

Over yonder, the onions tell tales,
Of basketball games where broccoli fails.
The cucumbers slide on a watery floor,
As a giant cabbage shouts, "Let's score!"

Fantasies sprout with a sprinkle of glee,
As carrots dream of climbing a tree.
In a patch full of laughter, oh what a sight,
Veggies at play, from morning till night.

So come, take a stroll through this fun,
Where every vegetable knows how to run.
The garden's alive with joy and good cheer,
In this world of green, there's nothing to fear.

The Enchanted Fragrance

The breeze carries scents of silly delight,
As daisies spill secrets under moonlight.
With laughter that tickles the tips of our noses,
The blooms crack jokes, making funny poses.

A lilac pretends it's a wise old sage,
While the peonies burst forth from their cage.
Whispers of sweetness, a fragrant charade,
In this garden, mischief is perfectly laid.

The night air is filled with giggles and cheer,
As blossoms pull pranks, drawing everyone near.
With petals that dance and tickle your toes,
This enchanted place, where hilarity grows.

So let's laugh with the flowers, revel in play,
As the fragrance of fun leads us astray.
In the magic of blooms, we'll frolic and roam,
In a scented wonderland, we'll always feel home.

Colorful Reflections

In a pond where the lilies wear bright crowns,
The frogs trade stories, sharing their frowns.
With splashes of color, they leap with delight,
Each jump brings a chuckle, oh what a sight!

Butterflies flutter, their wings so grand,
As daisies make daisy chains by hand.
The sun's a painter with a colorful brush,
In this garden parade, there's no need to rush.

A sunflower spins, declaring a dance,
While the petals stand still, lost in a trance.
Hilarity blooms in this mirthful place,
With laughter reflecting on each flower's face.

So gather 'round for this colorful spoil,
As joy takes the lead, and laughter we'll toil.
In the realm of bright hues and smiles galore,
Let's revel in fun, forever wanting more.

Meditations in Petal Form

In a patch of green, I found some charms,
Little purple hats that came with arms.
They raised a toast to the sun so bright,
Sipping dew drops, in morning light.

They whispered jokes to a passing bee,
As it buzzed along, feeling quite free.
"You think you're busy? Oh, what a thrill!"
"Try dodging raindrops, it's quite a skill!"

A snail slid by with a stylish grin,
"Slow and steady, now watch me win!"
The flowers laughed, petals in a whirl,
"C'mon, my friend, give life a twirl!"

So if you see the blooms so grand,
Join their party, take their hand.
Life's too short to sulk and frown,
Sway with the petals, dance around town.

Blossoms of Memory

In the garden of thoughts, a blip appears,
A flash of purple through the years.
Petals like laughter, soft and spry,
Tickling the nose of a passing fly.

Those wispy dreams in bloom's embrace,
Make giggles pop in curious space.
A clownfish wiggles through pastel hues,
While daisies whisper the funniest news.

"Oh dear snail, what do you see?"
"Not much," it mutters, "but you'll agree,
I'm the slowest in this race of fun,
But it's okay, the day's just begun!"

With each chuckle from the trees above,
I gather petals, wear my love.
For in this garden, where silliness thrives,
Memories blossom and laughter survives.

Twilight's Soft Secrets

As the day bids its cheeky adieu,
Violet skies giggle, with secrets anew.
The crickets chant in their silly song,
While the moon dips low, where its friends belong.

"Call the fireflies!" a blossom shouts,
"Let's light up the night, dispel the doubts!"
A worm juggles when no one's around,
Dreams twist and twirl on the chubby ground.

"Do you see that star, it winked at me?"
"Dear petals, it's just a mental spree,"
Laughter bubbles from shade to shine,
As twilight spins, in moments divine.

So here in the dusk, with laughter entwined,
We share our secrets, sweet and unrefined.
The night blooms forth with a comical sway,
As petals confide in the end of the day.

Dancing in the Lavender Fields

In fields of purple, joyfully wide,
The flowers host a dance with pride.
They twirl in rhythm, a jolly parade,
While bees join in, their buzzing cascade.

"Watch my moves!" says a cheeky sprout,
"I've got the best groove, no doubt!"
A breeze jumps in, with snickers and glee,
Tickling the flowers, oh, how carefree!

Then comes a ladybug wearing a hat,
"Who's the star here? I'm not that fat!"
The flowers chuckle, heads all a-bounce,
"Darling, it's you, come do another ounce!"

So together they jiggle and sway all around,
As laughter erupts from the lavender ground.
In this playful party, fun truly prevails,
In joyous embrace, where humor never fails.

Tapestry of Color and Light

In a field where colors play,
A purple patch plans to sway,
Socks mismatched, I skip and hop,
While butterflies giggle, 'Don't stop!'

A sunbeam draws a wiggly line,
Bumblebees buzzing, feeling fine,
I twirl, a dance on wobbly feet,
The grass below, oh so sweet!

With every giggle, petals burst,
My dance still leaves me quite immersed,
The colors laugh, they twist and twine,
In this silly world, all is divine.

So let's pluck joy, let's scoop delight,
A whimsical chase, oh what a sight!
In this tapestry, a cheerful thread,
We weave our laughter, onward we tread.

Visions Woven with Silk

Dreams unspool like threads in air,
With whimsy woven everywhere,
A squirrel in a bowler hat,
Dancing madly, imagine that!

Breezes tease with whispers light,
While mushrooms giggle in delight,
A tale unfolds in clumsy spritz,
Entwined in yarn, what a mix!

Laughter spools the tales we share,
In this land of silly flair,
With every twist, a chuckle flows,
We wear our joy like fancy clothes.

So look again, dear friend, and see,
How the world can be so free,
In vibrant hues and playful spins,
Life's a dance, it always wins!

Echoes Through the Garden

In the garden, giggles ring,
As daisies sway and frogs all sing,
A dapper toad in fancy dress,
Claims he's more than just a mess!

Sunflowers twist their funny faces,
Joking 'bout their local graces,
Petals tickle as I stroll,
In this magic, I'm the sole role!

The breeze carries a sweet refrain,
Squirrels play their nutty game,
A peek-a-boo with every glance,
In snapshots of this green romance.

So follow laughter, skip the doubt,
In this garden, shout it out,
With every echo, joy expands,
In nature's humor, life's grand plans.

The Art of Seeing

With kaleidoscope eyes, what a sight!
I paint the world in colors bright,
A clumsy brush, but what a laugh,
As silly squiggles take their path!

Bubbles float like dreams in air,
While kittens pounce without a care,
A comedy of paws and tails,
As laughter dances in the gales.

Each oddity a piece of art,
In the gallery of the heart,
Where blunders make the best of tales,
And joy rides high on laughter's trails.

So wear those colors, twirl around,
Embrace the silly, feel profound,
In every glance, the world's a spree,
This joyful mess is what we see!

Whispers of Lavender Dreams

In gardens where the mishaps bloom,
A dancing bee trips on its broom.
The flowers giggle, oh so spry,
As butterflies do the limbo high.

A squirrel tells a joke to a snail,
While a grasshopper recites a tale.
They chuckle loud beneath the sun,
While flowers swear they're just for fun.

A breezy gust starts a game of tag,
With petals floating, no need to brag.
The air is filled with bursts of glee,
As nature laughs with wild esprit.

So join the chatter, don't miss the play,
In this wacky world, let's laugh away.
For every bloom holds a tale indeed,
Where humor's the secret we all need.

Hues of Midnight Reverie

When shadows dance in shades of night,
The stars giggle at their own delight.
A bat wearing glasses flies like a drone,
Chasing moths who think they've grown.

The moon wears a hat, quite out of place,
While comets join in a cosmic race.
Each wink and nod from above the gloom,
Turns midnight into a vibrant room.

A fox paints stripes on all the trees,
Saying, "Look, I'm a zebra, if you please!"
While owls ponder life's great debate,
Is it better to hoot or to wait?

These nightly antics, oh what a thrill!
With laughter so loud, it brings a chill.
So let the stars spark joy in our heads,
As we prance with whimsy in our beds.

Petals Beneath the Moonlight

Under the glow of cheese-like beams,
The flowers plot outrageous schemes.
A daffodil dons a masquerade mask,
While roses do pirouettes—they bask!

With whispers that swirl like a gentle breeze,
The daisies gossip about summer's tease.
"Did you hear what a tulip wore?
A hat so big, it blocked the door!"

A tiny hedgehog shows off a dance,
In shoes made of leaves—oh what a chance!
They twirl and spin on the grass so green,
Creating a show fit for a queen.

As petals fall, they chuckle and leap,
Sowing laughter for everyone to keep.
In the moonlight's embrace, joy will unfold,
In a garden where laughter is pure gold.

Twilight's Fragrant Emanation

At twilight's door, the scents collide,
As giggling mint takes a slide.
Rosemary swoons with a wink and cheer,
Claiming, "This is my time of year!"

Lavender fluffs up, ready to strut,
While thyme does a jig, oh what a cut!
Each herb in a twist, a wacky parade,
Celebrating joy that never does fade.

The air is thick with a playful jest,
As basil shares recipes and a zest.
Chives crack up, they can barely stand,
"Join our fest, come eat our band!"

In twilight's glow, with laughter so sweet,
The garden's a stage, the world's our seat.
So let's raise a glass of fragrant mirth,
In this whimsical place, our joyful birth.

Tints of Solitude and Light

In the garden, whispers play,
Silly critters enjoying the day.
A snail with a hat, quite the sight,
Wearing laughter, a true delight.

The sunbeams dance, oh what a scene,
Chasing shadows, acting quite keen.
A bee in tights buzzes with flair,
While butterflies giggle, floating in air.

A worm in a tie gives a speech,
About how to wiggle and reach.
With wiggles and giggles, they cheer,
In this patch of glee, there's naught to fear.

So let the blooms chuckle and shine,
In a world where humor intertwines.
Where petals prance in the light,
And solitude's shades are whimsically bright.

Ethereal Blooms in the Mist

In a foggy patch, giggles abound,
Puppies chasing their tails all around.
A flower in polka dots, quite bizarre,
Sways to the rhythm of a kid's guitar.

Phantom giggles in the haze,
As mushrooms conspire with silliness plays.
A feathered hat on a sleeping frog,
Dreams of hopping, then a lazy slog.

The mist begins to twirl and swirl,
Caught in a dance, a whimsical whirl.
An owl with glasses pretends to teach,
While the dandelions tease with a peach.

Laughter echoes, soft and sweet,
As crickets tap a saucy beat.
In this cloudy realm, there's joy to find,
Where the ordinary is hilariously unconfined.

Murmurs of a Dreamt Horizon

Beyond the hills, where dreams do play,
A wave of giggles floats away.
Toadstools talk in riddles and rhymes,
As squirrels perform acrobatic climbs.

A floating pumpkin drifts with flair,
Chasing a breeze, oh what a dare!
With all its orange, a clownish guise,
Tickled by whispers of friendly skies.

The horizon winks, a cheeky grin,
While sunflowers tease and spin in a din.
A dancing hare, in slick little shoes,
Leads the parade with whimsical blues.

Round and round, the laughter runs,
In pockets of sun, bright as the sun.
Echoes delight in the fluffy white,
As daydreams twirl, just out of sight.

Dance of the Indigos

In twilight's glow, the fun begins,
With polka-dots and cheese grins.
A cat in socks struts with pride,
Chasing shadows that giggle and hide.

Indigo petals wave with flair,
While a raccoon sneaks a picnic to share.
With crumbs of laughter crackling bright,
Their goofy antics light up the night.

A skunk in a tutu twirls and prances,
As fireflies join in glowing dances.
The moon takes a chuckle-filled leap,
Keeping secrets that critters keep.

With every giggle and silly spin,
Nature's joy shines from within.
Dancing through hues of laughter so sweet,
In this world where whimsy can't be beat.

Hues of Intuition

In a garden where whispers run,
Colors dance, just look at the fun.
A purple hue, a yellow tinge,
What's that smell? It makes me cringe!

Silly petals play hide and seek,
Tickling noses, oh so meek.
A flower knows, but won't reveal,
What's brewing near, what's the deal?

Bumblebees buzz, they trip and roll,
Dressing dandelions like a troll.
A bouquet laughs with rays of sun,
Who knew that petals could be such fun?

In a world where colors peak,
Nonsense blooms, rare and unique.
So join the pageant, dance in air,
Floral jokes, without a care!

Mysteries Written in Petals

In the garden, the flowers scheme,
Each petal holds a secret dream.
A daisy blinks, a rose just sighs,
What's hidden now beneath the skies?

A tulip whispers tales from night,
Of buttercups in their yellow light.
What do they think, those sneaky blooms?
Are they scheming? Do they zoom?

With colors bright, they plot and play,
In the cool breezes of the day.
Gather 'round where stories dwell,
Flowery gossip, oh so swell!

So if you hear a giggle near,
It's just the blossoms, have no fear.
They'll tickle your heart, with laughs they toss,
For every petal, a mystery gloss!

Chasing Twilight's Embrace

As the day drifts to its close,
The garden winks, the moonlit rose.
Dancing shadows on the ground,
Steps of whimsy all around!

Lavender giggles, shows its flair,
While daisies twirl without a care.
Oh, what a sight! A sight to see,
In this flower-led jubilee!

The twilight hums a playful tune,
As blossoms begin to swoon.
A daisy smirks, "Is this a dream?"
While crickets join in with a beam!

So let's embrace this twilight charm,
With flutters that will keep us warm.
Chasing night in floral delight,
Where laughter dances with the light!

Fragrance of Hope

A whiff of joy hangs in the air,
With every bloom, they shed a stare.
An aroma of giggles rushes by,
Is it laughter, or a sly pie?

In the meadow, scents twirl and spin,
Whose perfume is that? Let's jump in!
With each petal, a cheer will rise,
A fragrant hug beneath the skies.

Oh, tulips tease with their bright cheer,
While violets wink, "Come closer, dear."
With playful scents and jolly sings,
Life's a flower party—who brings the flings?

So breathe it in, the playful air,
Hope's fragrance blooms; it's everywhere.
In a world of smiles, soft and wide,
Nature laughs; come join the ride!

Ethereal Threads

In a garden where socks go to dance,
Gnomes trade secrets, they take a chance.
With mismatched shoes and hats askew,
They sip on tea, and giggle too.

The daisies gossip, oh what a scene,
While butterflies plan their next cuisine.
A pickle reveals it's quite the sage,
As daisies blush on the gossip stage.

Celestial Blooms

Stars sprinkle glitter on tulip hats,
A raccoon waltzes with garden spats.
Giggling lilies, in shades of green,
Join a conga line, oh what a scene!

The sun beams down, plays peekaboo,
While daisies dance in the morning dew.
A fern rolls over, tickled by breeze,
And origami frogs croak 'more, please!'

Journey through the Blue Shadows

Wandering through hues of sapphire light,
A squirrel in pajamas takes flight!
Chasing shadows, tippy-toe,
Stumbling over a sleepy toad, oh no!

Mistakes are made on this magical ride,
With laughter echoing far and wide.
A sunflower snickers – what a funny sight,
As the moon giggles, "You'll be alright!"

A Canvas of Floral Dreams

Brushes dipped in lemonade,
Paint the day in a lively parade.
Squirrels with berets twirl and spin,
While daisies strike a pose, let the fun begin!

Marigolds chuckle at a lost hat,
While bumblebees dance in a chatty spat.
They argue over colors, dark and bright,
As snickers ripple through the warm twilight.

Recollections in Bloom

In a garden where the odd balls grow,
A bee danced in a fancy toe.
With lavender shoes and a bright bowtie,
He twirled on petals, oh my, oh my!

A squirrel played a trumpet with flair,
As daisies giggled—what a vibrant affair!
The sun wore glasses and lounged for a tan,
While squirrels debated who's the best fan.

A snail on a skateboard zipped by with glee,
Crying, 'I'm fast, but it's hard to be me!'
With mayhem and laughter, the blooms start to sway,
In this whimsical world, we're all here to play.

So let's toss our hats and prance like the breeze,
In this enchanting bazaar, we do just as we please!
A realm where moments are painted with cheer,
Oh, what a time, with no worries, my dear!

Palette of the Soul's Embrace

In a shop where hues come alive,
A paintbrush does jiggles, and colors connive.
The blues chat with yellows, laughing so bright,
While reds declare, 'We own the spotlight!'

A canvas pretending it's part of the crew,
Wobbles and giggles, but claims it's just blue.
'Oh why do they swirl? Can't they see I'm so still?'
Everyone chuckles—it's part of the thrill!

A palette with colors too proud to blend,
Argue for hours—no way will they bend.
The green screams for nature, the pink begs for fun,
While orange just juggles, eyeing the sun.

In this madcap circus of pigment delight,
Each shade prances 'til day turns to night.
So grab your brush, and let's dance on the plain,
In this chaotic carnival, we're free from all pain!

Murmurs from the Indigo Depths

In the echoes of shadows, a fish sings a tune,
With sparkles of laughter that drift 'round the moon.
A crab with a monocle counts all the shells,
While jellyfish float, painting whimsical spells.

Octopus chefs whip up pickles and pies,
Winking at seahorses who wear silly ties.
A whale cracks a joke, causing ripples of cheer,
While the underwater crowd shouts, 'More, we want beer!'

A starfish in glasses reads funny novels,
As currents bring gossip; oh, how it wobbles!
The seas are alive with a splash and a giggle,
As squids swing their tentacles, oh, how they wiggle!

So dive in the depths, where laughter must bloom,
In this quirky world, there's always more room.
With bubbles and chuckles, they dance 'neath the waves,
In the ocean of joy, everyone craves!

The Garden of Lost Horizons

In a patch where the oddest of weeds come to play,
A gnome in a tutu leads ballet every day.
With worms as their partners and daisies on high,
They pirouette wildly and leap to the sky.

A frog wearing glasses recites ancient lore,
While ants build a tower just to show off their score.
The sun yawns and stretches with a grin on its face,
As flowers debate if they've run out of space.

One tree tells the tale of the squirrels it knows,
Who often wear helmets when riding on crows.
They grip their small nuts (not what you think, dear),
And chuckle at others now filled up with cheer.

So wander this garden, where every nose giggles,
And truths take a tumble, while laughter just wriggles.
With whimsy and wonder, let us all roam,
In this riotous haven, we're awfully at home!

The Spirit of Blossoming

In gardens where laughter takes flight,
Butterflies giggle, oh what a sight!
Petals dance slightly, tickling the air,
As daisies snicker without a care.

A sunflower wears a comical grin,
While tulips shove each other to win.
The breeze carries jokes from bloom to bloom,
Filling the field with whimsical gloom.

Even the bees can't stop their cheer,
Buzzing to rhythms so silly and clear.
Nature's own comedy, a vibrant display,
In this merry garden, we all want to play.

So come join the fun, don't be shy,
With petals and giggles that reach for the sky!
In a world where flowers can crack a good pun,
The Spirit of Blossoming is second to none.

Melodies of the Floral Mind

In a meadow where whispers collide,
The blooms turn their heads, full of pride.
They hum silly songs, a floral delight,
As bees tap their feet, a marvelous sight.

A rose sings sweet, but adds a sly pun,
While daisies chuckle, "Is this really fun?"
Lilies laugh hard, petals shaking in glee,
Creating a chorus, so wild and free.

Pansies parade in their colorful hues,
Telling tall tales of the night's funny snooze.
The flora's a band, with no need for a stage,
Just nature's jokes, turning every page.

So let's dance along and let out a cheer,
For the melodies bloom when good humor's near!
With laughter and fragrance, together we sway,
In the Melodies of the Floral Mind, we play.

Threads of Nightshade

In the twilight, where shadows creep,
The nightshade giggles, never in sleep.
Its petals weave tales of laughter and jest,
As funny little sprites put humor to test.

Crickets are cackling, a musical show,
While moths join the fun, with their delicate glow.
The moon winks down, a sly little grin,
As nightshade whispers, "Let the fun begin!"

Dancing, they twirl, in a colorful spree,
With cosmic confetti drifting carefree.
The stars roll their eyes, and chuckle away,
At the wild antics that steal the day.

Such is the magic, when darkness takes flight,
Where laughter weaves through the fabric of night.
In Threads of Nightshade, we find our delight,
With giggles and jests, oh what a sight!

The Color of Whispers

In the hush of the field where secrets convene,
The whispers are painted in colors unseen.
With each chuckle, a hue takes its place,
Blushing bright with a comical grace.

The violet grins, with a snicker so bold,
While primroses chuckle, their stories retold.
Every breeze carries giggles so sly,
As petals get carried up high in the sky.

A patch of bright laughter takes root in the soil,
While snickering petals take joy in their toil.
Each hue adds a punchline, a twist in the tale,
In a garden where humor will always prevail.

So come seek the joy in whispers of hue,
Where laughter blooms brightly, painting the view.
In the Color of Whispers, let laughter take flight,
And together we'll relish the joy of the night.

Celestial Blooms Unfurled

In a field of purple snacks,
Flowers giggle, close your racks.
Butterflies wear tiny shoes,
Dancing 'round the garden blues.

Bees are buzzing high on sugar,
Sipping tea and that's not chugger.
Sunflowers wear their favorite hats,
While rabbits plan to steal the mats.

Worms throw parties in the dirt,
In their finest suits, all inurt.
Raining jellybeans from above,
It's a world of silly love!

So if you stumble on this place,
Don't forget to dance with grace.
Join the blooms in joyful jest,
And laugh away your daily quest!

Echoes in the Garden

A squirrel sings a tune off key,
To marigolds, oh can't you see?
A dandelion rolls its eyes,
As daisies pluck their petals, why!

Chickens wear a crown of leaves,
Wobbling like they're on the breeze.
Tomatoes share their gossip tales,
While cucumbers don pirate sails.

Here, the tulips play charades,
As rabbits guard their carrot parades.
Laughter echoes 'midst the greens,
In this patch, joy reigns supreme.

So gather round, join the mirth,
For in this patch, there's endless worth.
When flowers giggle and sway just right,
You'll find humor, pure delight!

Glistening Shadows of Sorrow

In the gloom of gloomy nights,
There's a gnome painting silly sights.
Puddles laugh, reflecting woe,
While shadows play a game of show.

The moon's downing a cupcake treat,
While crickets bring the dancing beat.
Sad plants hum a muted tune,
Wishing they could fly to the moon.

Yet in every droop and pout,
A giggle sneaks its way about.
For even shadows have their fun,
In a garden where jokes are spun.

So if you find a tear or two,
Just tickle them and start anew.
For every gloom holds laughter near,
In glistening shades, the jest is clear!

The Palette of Distant Memories

Once a flower donned a shoe,
Riding on a snail, how 'bout you?
A breeze said, 'What a silly sight!'
While clouds giggled, pure delight.

In fields where colors blend and play,
A rainbow butterfly flies away.
It swaggers, tipping its tiny hat,
Chasing memories of a fuzzy cat.

Petunias swap their pastel tales,
While lavender dons its fancy veils.
Old gnomes reminisce of days so bright,
When laughter bloomed from morning light.

So take a stroll through memory's lane,
Find the colors, dance in the rain.
For every hue brings joy anew,
In this palette of yesteryear's view!

www.ingramcontent.com/pod-product-compliance
Lightning Source LLC
Chambersburg PA
CBHW071838160426
43209CB00003B/342